JUDGEMENT OF THE NATIONS

Prophecy of
Matthew 25:31-46
(Sheep and Goats)

Saul P. Cortez

Foreword

It is unknown when Matthew wrote his gospel, the best guess according to the commentary is somewhere between the 40's and the 70's AD. I opt for the early 40's and tend to believe that Matthew being a collector of taxes for the Romans had numerous associations among them. Moreover, even if he wrote for a Jewish audience as it is supposed, his Gospel along with this particular prophecy of the "division of Gentile sheep and goats" was probably well known among his former colleagues as the gospel spread across the Empire. This prophetic warning for Gentile eyes and ears on the consequences of rejecting Jesus' "brethren" was no doubt the main reason for its rendering. A secondary reason, yet of no less importance was for our eyes today and there are very good reasons for this. In addition, this is not parroting of "futurist" stale material which regards all prophetic events, including this one, as still unfulfilled. A view point which I do not believe Scripture agrees with. Therefore, if you have had unanswered questions after reading dispensationalist/futurist material, then I believe this fantastic little book will bring you into the light of day.

The Author

Verse 31

"But when the Son of Man comes _in His glory_"

The significance of this text is that at this point of "His coming," Jesus is already "glorified" or as the text reads, He comes "in His glory." This is in keeping with the context of His request to the Father in the gospel of John.

"And now glorify me together with Thyself, Father, with the glory which I had with You before the world was." (John 17:5).

We can rightly assume that His request was granted and that at His resurrection or upon His ascension entered once again into the "glory He had with the Father before the world was." Hence, the reading of verse 31 above correctly states (He) "comes in His glory." As we will explain in detail later when we take up the last part of this verse the word "glory" is the Greek word "doxa" which implies "being recognized" for who one is. The Lord returned into heaven and into His "glory/recognition," a "glory" which of course implies power, authority, majesty, and everything else God is.

Verse 31A

"And all His _angels_ with Him."

Angels" is the Greek word 'Aggelos' and in English it is the word 'messengers.

3

According to the - Lexical Aids to the New Testament, "Angel - is not a name of nature but of office, or human messenger." Though it is possibly speaking of heavenly angels, it more likely refers to believers.

Vine's Expository Dictionary of Bible Words has this to say of the term 'angel,' "the word itself primarily means 'messenger.' The term refers to the human and the divine."

Human Messengers - Angels in the Bible.

Matthew 11:10 "Behold I sent my (angel) messenger before your face." (Also Mark 1:2) (John Baptist)
Revelation 1:20 "The seven stars are the angels of the seven churches." (Pastors of the churches.)
Philippians 2:25 "Epaphroditus, my brother and fellow worker, who is also your messenger (angel) and minister to my need."
James 2:25 "Rahab was justified when she received the (angels) messengers."

The book of the "Revelation of Jesus Christ" was given (shown in symbols) to John to give the Churches a "preview" of "the things which are (were) and the things which shall take place after these things." (Revelation 1:19). This was a "revealing" to John and indirectly to the Churches. However, when the Scriptures speak of the Lord Jesus being "revealed from heaven" such as the following example, it was a (subjective) revealing to the whole of the Roman Empire.

"When the Lord Jesus <u>shall be revealed</u> from heaven with His mighty angels (messengers) in flaming fire, dealing out retribution to those who do not know God and to those who do not obey the gospel of our Lord Jesus, these will pay the penalty of eternal destruction." 2 Thessalonians 1:7

4

This occurs during the period of AD 66 through 73; known as "The Great Tribulation" The fiery judgment that the "angels" brought forth at the time had two aspects to it. One aspect was "literal" or physical, which were the Roman legions invading Israel in AD 66, with "flaming fire' they burned Jerusalem and the Jewish Temple by AD 70. While the brunt of the "Tribulation" was suffered by the nation of Israel, (Daniel 12:1, 7), there was judgment throughout the Roman provinces as civil war ensued and ravaged the entire empire. The civil war brought about Nero's suicide on, 9 June 68 and lasted until mid to late AD 69 when Flavius Vespasian was proclaimed Emperor. The second aspect of this judgment was the "revealing of the Lord Jesus." How the "Tribulation" "revealed Jesus" is readily clear when we understand that the word "reveal" which is the Greek word 'apokalupsis' is used in Scripture subjectively and objectively.

"Vine's Complete Expository Dictionary." (Page 531-532)
Reveal – "The NT occurrences of this word fall under two heads, subjective and objective. The subjective is that in which something is presented to the mind directly."

Therefore, the invasion of the Roman Legions into Judea (Matthew 24:16) exactly as prophesied by the OT prophets and than by Jesus and subsequently by the disciples "revealed Jesus," who was in heaven, "subjectively." This "revealing" through fulfillment of prophecy was not so much for the disciples who already believed but primarily for the entire Roman Empire population who was well aware and in many cases tired of hearing about the coming wrath/judgment of the God of Israel. This extraordinary fulfillment of a prediction all the empire had heard for at least thirty-three years vividly "revealed Jesus" to them. The "revealing" was not "objective," they did not see the Lord with their physical eyes but rather "subjective they "saw" with their understanding.

This "revealing" of Jesus to all the civilized world of that time brought Jesus the "glory" (recognition) that he was truly God Almighty! "In this way every eye saw Him," you see. This is true even for present day believers where this "recognition" or "glory" has traversed the centuries and causes us to believe on Him today.

This is the reason why the lord said, **"This gospel shall be preached in the whole "world" for a witness."** (Matthew 24:14). "World" is not the Greek word 'kosmos' which means entire planet or universe, but rather the Greek word is 'oikoumene' which refers to the Roman Empire, (see Luke 2:1). The gospel message until AD 66 across the Empire was "Repent and believe the gospel for the 'end' (of the age) is near and the wrath of God according to the Law of Moses will sweep across the empire, especially in Judea, with "flaming fire." The entire population of the Empire "witnessed" or we could say it as John did in Revelation 1:7, "Every eye will see Him." The trouble with some folks is that they expect every prophecy to be physical especially the 'parousia' (presence) which is a "coming" to be with His people but not physically. These folks like to call themselves "Literalists" as if spiritual fulfillments were not literal. Israel of old made the same mistake including both Pharisees and Sadducees.

Some other texts where "reveal" is used subjectively: A revelation to men's minds and hearts.

Matthew 11:27
Philippians 3:15
Ephesians 3:5
1 Peter 1:12

As I said earlier, there were two aspects to the "flaming fiery" judgment. The first as we mentioned was the physical Roman burning of Jerusalem and the temple along with the great devastation of human life, over one million unbelieving Jews, Idumeans, and other Jewish proselytes slaughtered. The second aspect was the spiritual. Which included the "casting into the "lake of Fire" (Revelation 20:15). You will note Paul mentions this in addition to the "flaming fire" in 2nd Thessalonians, "these will pay the penalty of eternal destruction."

Verse 31b

"Then He will sit on His glorious throne (place of being recognized as King)." (NAS)

The "Literal Concordant Version" says, "Than He shall be seated on the throne of His glory, (recognition or be recognized), on the earth. Paraphrased – "Than He shall be seen in His proper place as King of kings and Lord of lords.

As Paul tells Timothy,
Glory = # 1391, Doxa "to recognize a person or thing for what it is."

Therefore, what verse 31 actually says is "When Jesus comes to be recognized by the world for who he is." Has Jesus been "recognized" for who He is? There may be many who would answer no this question. However, that is not true for Jesus has been "recognized" across the centuries by millions and today by billions. At the time of fulfillment of this prophecy in Matthew, between the years 66 through 73 there were thousands of believers.

7

Afterward and up to the year 300, they multiplied so fast that Emperor Constantine was forced to "recognize" Jesus as Lord and Savior and Christianity as the official religion of the Empire. Today, the name of Jesus is glorified and He is worshiped all over the globe! Therefore, the answer to the question is an unequivocal yes! Those who say no do so because they are looking at the half of the glass which is empty. They do this because they have been persuaded into believing that the world has to be squeaky-clean from "sin" and everyone physically kneeling at the feet of Jesus before they believe that he is "recognized." Granted, much work remains to be done. However, contrary to Dispensationalism which says that the Lord wins at the end, the Lord is always in the winners circle! The way they teach it, the Lord and His people are battered, bruised, and bleeding for three whole quarters and fourteen minutes of the fourth but pull out a victory in the last minute.

We must be cognizant and never lose sight of the fact that Jesus must have come to be "recognized" ("glorified") for whom He was by the AD 66-73 invasion of Israel. Jesus proclaimed during His earthly ministry the coming wrath (judgment) of Israel in particular and for the entire Roman Empire generally, (Matthew 24). The disciples proclaimed the same from AD 33 and until at least the beginning of the Roman invasion in AD 66. In fact, the 1st century disciples who walked with the Lord are verily discredited today by futurist "prophecy-experts" for this very thing and ridiculed by unbelievers as being confused and in the dark as to the "end of the age." Their fundamental and constant message for at least thirty-three years was, "Jesus is the Messiah of the world who has paid for our sins. Therefore, repent and believe the gospel for there is an Empire-wide judgment of the wrath of God coming in our generation."

They made statements such as the following.

Romans 16:20 **"The God of peace will <u>soon</u> crush Satan under your feet."**

1 Corinthians 10:11 **"They were written for our instruction, <u>upon whom the ends of the age have come.</u>"**

1st Peter 4:7 **"The end of all things is <u>at hand.</u>"**

Hebrews 9:26 "But now once at the consummation (end) of the ages, He (Jesus) has been manifested to put away sin by the sacrifice of Himself."

Below is what the **"Lexical Aids to the New Testament" in the Hebrew – Greek Key Study Bible"** has to say about the word "end" as used above.

"The word **"ends"** and **"end"** in the above texts is the Greek word 'Telos.' This word does not, as is commonly supposed, mean the extinction, end, or termination, with reference to time, but the goal reached the completion or conclusion at which anything arrives." (End of quote)

However, according to "futurists," aided by their "prophecy-experts" these texts do refer to a future end, extinction, and or termination, of time, as we know it. In other words, contrariwise to Scripture they are saying the end of the physical universe is in mind in these texts! It is mind-boggling to think that some of these brothers actually graduated out of seminaries. I have all the respect for education however, if one starts with a crooked measuring stick one winds up with a crooked house. Take a gander at the word **"appearing"** below.

"Until the <u>appearing</u> of our Lord Jesus Christ, which He will bring about at the proper time - He who is the blessed and only Sovereign, the King of kings and Lord of lords. (First Timothy 6:14-15) (NAS)

"Appearing" is the Greek word 'Epiphaneia' which literally means – "<u>to appear glorious.</u>" This is exactly what occurred when prophecy was fulfilled before the very eyes of the entire population of the Roman Empire. Whether they accepted Christ as their Lord or not they "recognized Him." They literally saw the words of Jesus and His disciples come to pass. I would think that many exclaimed like the centurion on Mount Calvary, "Truly this was the Son of God" (Matthew 27:54). Christ indeed was "manifested" "appeared glorious," or "in His glory" Due spiritually and physically speaking to this manifestation of prophecy by AD 306, the Church rose from the one hundred and twenty to literally dominate the entire landscape of the most brutal military/political power ever known to man and that without sword or shield.

Verse 32

"And all the nations will be gathered before Him."

"Nations" – "Ethnos" this refers to all the nationalities under the Roman banner besides Judaism. I believe Matthew 25:1-13 (The ten virgins) is the prophecy concerning the Jews at the "end of the age." (Our catalog contains a teaching on CD about the "Ten Virgins.") Three other places in the NT speak to this "gathering of nations" before Him.

One is found in Matthew 13:47-51.
"Again, the kingdom of heaven is like a dragnet cast into the sea, and gathering of every kind; and when it was filled. They drew it up on the beach; and they sat down; and gathered the good into containers, but the bad (rotten) they threw away." So it will be at the end of the age; the angels shall come forth, and take out the wicked from among the righteous, and will cast them into the furnace of fire; there will be weeping and gnashing of teeth."** (This is comparable with the judgment in Matthew 25:31-46.)

Another is Second Corinthians 5:10.
"For we must all "appear" before the judgment seat of Christ to be recompensed for the deeds in the body, whether good or bad."

"Appear" – the Greek here is 'phaneroo'. "Refers to those to whom the revelation is made." (As opposed to 'apokalupto' which refers only to the object being revealed.) This "judgment seat" I believe is most likely associated with the "parable of the talents" (Matthew 25:14-30). This "slaves" or servants of the Lord are the Jewish believers in particular but includes Gentile Christians as well.

The third text is Revelation 20:12
"And I saw the dead, the great and the small, standing before the throne, and books were opened; and another book was opened, which is of life; and the dead were judged from the things which were written in the books, according to their deeds."

"Dead" is the Greek word 'nekros,' used in the NT as an adjective to describe a body as dead or as a noun rendered as "the dead." Here in Revelation it is a noun.

11

We must take caution in reaching conclusions when we run across the word as it is used in different ways. Some of us interpret the word rigidly believing rigidity to be a Godly virtue. We need to learn the difference between resolute and obstinate. Without spiritual revelation, we can be stubborn when we need to be pliable. Paul informs us that as unbelievers we were "dead in trespasses and sins" (Ephesians 2:1). However, Paul also turned around and wrote believers telling them the following.

"Now if we have <u>died</u> with Christ we believe that we shall also live with Him." (Romans 6:8)

Again to the Romans,
"And if Christ is in you, though <u>the body is "dead"</u> because of sin." (Romans 8:10)

This may be confusing to many and indeed has been. When we rightly divide Scripture, that is interpret it correctly, we began to see how Paul used 'dead" "death" and "dying" in a spiritual sense. What do I mean? To start with, let's look at the two texts above. We are informed By Paul who received it by revelation that a believer upon receiving Christ "died." Earlier in the chapter, he writes, "do you not know that all of us who have been baptized into Christ Jesus have been baptized into His 'death" (Romans 6:3). We of course know that in physical reality believers were not dead! Therefore, the "death" Paul spoke of was a spiritual reality. The "body" that had "died" refers to the soul man, "first Adam," his being consisted of soul and body, (Genesis 2:7). Paul refers to this "soul man" as "**our <u>old man</u> who was crucified with Christ**" (Romans 6:6). He (the first Adam) "died" soul and body on the cross spiritually speaking but Paul uses the word "body" to refer to him.

This "body," this first Adam, this soul man, was to be "quickened" "made alive," spiritually speaking of course, bringing about.

"The abolishing of the last enemy, (death)." (1 Corinthians 15:26).

This happened when sin was dealt with at the judgment of Israel AD 66-73, because:

"The sting of death is sin, and the power of sin is the law" (1 Corinthians 15:56).

Thus, the law was fulfilled eliminating the last vestiges of the "Law of sin and "death" (Romans 8:2). Therefore, believers and unbelievers were all considered "dead" though believers were "alive in spirit." When the Scripture tells us, "Christ was the first-born from "the dead" (Colossians 1:18) it is letting us know that on Resurrection Sunday, Jesus was the first being to be born-again; everyone else at the time, the entire creation was "dead," spiritually speaking.

Verse 32b

"He will separate them from one another, as the shepherd separates the sheep from the goats. As the shepherd separates the sheep from the goats."

This is a spiritual separation of Gentile believers and unbelievers. Believers are gathered into the kingdom of life and the "goats are severed off into continual spiritual death. This prophecy is not to be confused with the "Tares and the wheat." That parable I believe is restricted to Israel.

13

The church in Jerusalem was infiltrated by "false brethren" (Galatians 2:4). You will notice that the parable says the "wheat and the tares were seemingly growing out together." (Matthew 13:26). When the servants of the landowner in the parable offer to "take out the tares" (28) the landowner responds that it is best to wait until harvest (AD 70) "lest you root out the wheat with the tares" (29). This occurred at the outset of the invasion into Israel by Roman Legions "the wheat" (believers), being warned in Matthew 24:15-16, fled out of Judea. The "tares" remained to be **"cast into the fire."**

Verse 33

"He will put the sheep on His right and the goats on His left."

"A wise man's heart directs him toward the right, but the foolish man's heart directs him toward the left." (Ecclesiastes 10:2)
I do not know how this prophetic word came about but it is right on.

"In thy right hand there are pleasures forever more." (Psalm 16:11)

"Thy right hand is full of righteousness." (Psalm 48:10)

"When Jesus had made purification of sins, He sat down at the right hand of the Majesty on high." (Hebrews 1:3)

Verse 34

"Then <u>the King</u> will say to those on His right, Come, you who are blessed of My Father, <u>inherit the kingdom</u> prepared for you from the foundation of the world."

The "kingdom" is the inheritance. Salvation is physically symbolized in the O. T. by the coming out of Egypt by the strong arm of God. The inheritance on the other hand has to do with crossing Jordan and entering the "Promised Land." Even as it took forty years from Egypt to Israel crossing Jordan, so it was from the Cross to the Church entering the Kingdom. God by His right hand saved us in AD 33 and set up His Kingdom at the conclusion of the judgment of Israel in AD 73. Paul writes about the entering into the kingdom.

"Flesh and blood cannot have inheritance in the kingdom" (First Corinthians 15:50)

What does Paul mean? Paul was not saying that our physical bodies would have "no inheritance" in the kingdom for indeed they do. There is healing and strength for our bodies in the kingdom. However, the kingdom is "not of this world" (John 18:36). It is not of a physical nature, it is spiritual! Therefore, in the literal and physical sense, our biological bodies, made of dust, do not "inherit the kingdom." However, what Paul is saying is that the "image of the heavenly" (spirit-man) would have no place for natural/soulish, "First Adam" type life which walks according to the five senses and not the spirit! If one was to partake of the kingdom, it had to be on spiritual terms through revelation, not human reasoning. In verse, forty-one below we will discuss how our "body of sin" (soul-man) was taken to the cross by the Lord and how afterwards as Paul explains it is "quickened" or "made alive" at the resurrection.

Inheritance

Scripture illustrates that forgiveness of sins and inheritance are two different blessings.

"In Christ we have redemption through His blood, the forgiveness of our sins, according to the riches of His grace." (Ephesians 1:7)

Four verses later, Paul writes:

"In whom <u>also</u> we have obtained an inheritance, having been predestinated according to His purpose" (Ephesians 1:11).

In the Epistle which Paul wrote to the brethren at Rome, He enlightens them to the truth that Abraham or his "Seed" (Christ) was the "heir" of the "world," (Kosmos/Universe). (Romans 4:13).

In fact, all the promises of eternal consequence were all made to Abraham's "Seed" (See Genesis 17:1-8). Moreover, I am glad that God saw fit to have Paul amplify on this important matter when he writes the Galatia church. Paul writes that contrary to what Jews believe the promises to Abraham were to Christ, not to Israel. Many Christians today inducted into the "Israel is still chosen" school of thought align themselves with right-wing Israelites who indulge in "a tooth for a tooth and an eye for an eye mentality."

(Here is what Paul wrote about the promises to Abraham.) **"Now the promises were spoken to Abraham and to his seed, He does not say, "And to seeds," as to many, but to one, "And to your seed," that is, Christ."** (Galatians 3:16)

Therefore, Christ is "heir of all" Paul also informs us that, "As children of God, we are heirs also, heirs of God and fellow heirs with Christ" (Romans 8:17). Just as we see that the children of Israel upon coming into the "promised land" along with conflicts and battles, received houses, money, fields, cattle, sheep. The kingdom promised much more.

"The blessing of Abraham"

"In order that in Christ Jesus the blessing of Abraham might come to the Gentiles, so that we might receive the promise of the Spirit." (Galatians 3:14)

What is the "blessing of Abraham?" To understand this we need to go to Abraham's time.

"God took Abram outside and said, "Now look toward the heavens and count the stars, if you are able to count them." Moreover, He said to him, "So shall your <u>seed</u> (singular) become. " Than Abram believed in the Lord; and the Lord <u>reckoned it to Abram as righteousness</u>." (Genesis 15:5-6)

This was the blessing! It is needful to stop and grasp the grandeur of this. Abram, later renamed Abraham by the Lord, became the first "righteous man" until his "seed" Jesus Christ was born in Bethlehem. The promises were all made to Abraham and "his seed," which is Christ." When you and I accepted Jesus, the "seed" of Abraham, as Savior and Lord we received righteousness. This made us the "sinless vessel" necessary to receive the "Holy Spirit" into our lives. So what happens when we receive the Holy Spirit?

Access

"For through Christ both Jewish and Gentile believers have access <u>in one Spirit</u> to the Father. (Ephesians 2:18) "Through Jesus Christ we have obtained access by faith <u>into this grace</u>." (Romans 5:2)

"Grace" = "Unearned and unmerited favor"
You and I as Christians have unlimited access into the unsearchable riches of Christ. We have unlimited access by faith into this grace (favor). ""All things are now possible to him that believes." Jesus operated under kingdom principles and in kingdom authority.

From the baptism at Jordan until AD 33 and His arrest, the Lord walked under kingdom authority. Demons, nature, sickness, sins, all were under His authority. The followers He commissioned were given authority, for instance, the twelve, and the seventy. Jesus came with authority and could delegate it even though He was not yet the ruling power in the universe. So how could Jesus operate under authority if He was not the "ruler?" Because Jesus was not of the "first Adam" and it was the "first Adam" who was under bondage. Adam and his linage were **"sold into bondage to sin"** (Romans 7:14). **"He (the ruler) who had the power of death, that is the devil"** (Hebrews 2:14) had tried to bring the Lord into that bondage but unsuccessfully, (Matthew 4). Therefore, Jesus could say, **"But he has nothing in me"** (John 14:30). Even though **"God sent His own Son in the likeness of sinful flesh"** (Romans 8:3) that is "free will" (the freedom to sin) and tempted **"in all points as we are, yet remained without sin"** (Hebrews 4:15).

From the day of Pentecost AD 33, until the Judgment of Israel AD 70, all believers operated under kingdom authority and principles in the name of Jesus Christ, because Jesus said, **"all authority in heaven and earth has been given unto me, go ye therefore"** (Matthew 28:18). However, a piece of work remained to be accomplished before the kingdom itself could be established on the earth. It was like when Eisenhower and the Allied Forces landed in Normandy on D-Day. They may have had all the authority, both moral, from God, and political from the French Government in exile, but the Allied flag was still not flying in Paris or Berlin. There was **"a last enemy yet to be destroyed,"** (1st Corinthians 15:26).

When Israel, the vessel of Law, was finally judged (AD 66-73) and that Covenant done away with, then was fulfilled. **"They all will become old as a garment, and as a mantle Thou will roll them up"** (Hebrews 1:11). The law was called the "ministry of death" by none other than the apostle Paul, (2nd Corinthians 3:7). The **"Law is spiritual, holy, righteous, and good"** (Romans 7:12, 14) however, **"no one is justified by the Law,** (Galatians 3:11). With Israel and its Levitical order of sacrifices done away with, the kingdom was set up on the earth "in the days of those kings" (Roman), and "it will endure forever" (Daniel 2:44, and 7:27).

Verse 35-36

"For I was hungry, and you gave me to eat; I was thirsty, and you gave me drink; I was a stranger, and you invited me in; naked, and you clothed me; I was sick, and you visited me; I was in prison, and you came to me."

The truth that Jesus is pressing here is gospel-related and not social-activism as most are wont to believe. To be sure, the terms "hungry, thirsty, stranger, naked, sick, in prison," are to be taken literally, perhaps "naked," not entirely. However, it is to whom these terms refer which gives this "judgment" its precise meaning. Knowing the precise meaning will also give us the precise time of its occurrence, something we will shortly see. The Lord says He was hungry, thirsty, naked, sick, and in prison, which provoked a question.

Verses 37-39

The Questions

"Then the <u>righteous</u> will answer Him, saying, Lord, when did we see you hungry, and feed you, or thirsty, and give you drink? When did we see you a stranger, and invite you in, or naked, and clothe you? When did we see you sick, or in prison, and come to you?

Paul informs us:
"We are the body of Christ and individually members of it. (2nd Corinthians 12:27)

"The church which is His body." (Ephesians 1:23)

"Christ in you (us) the hope of glory." (Colossians 1:27)

The Lord related this prophesies to the disciples with the intent that they would note them and pass them on. The fact that the Lord calls those on His right "righteous" would reveal to the hearer and later the reader their identity. What the Lord said next spells out to the hearer the Lord's intent for this foretelling of future judgment events.

Verse 40

"The king will answer and say to them, truly I say to you, to the extent that you did it unto one of <u>these my brethren</u>, even the least of them, you did it to me."

<u>Two examples below of whom Jesus referred to as brethren.</u>

Matthew 28:10) **"Then Jesus said to them, Do not be afraid; go and take word to <u>my brethren</u> to leave for Galilee, and there they shall see me."**

John 20:17) **"But go to <u>my brethren</u> and say to them, I ascend to my Father and your Father, and my God and your God."**

    The way that the Lord has the "returning king" answer the "sheep" is most interesting and enlightening. Jesus was walking out of Jerusalem speaking of future events to His disciples, the Twelve, plus others. Beginning with this chapter (25), Jesus begins to paint pictures in words. First, two parables, "the ten virgins" and "the talents," and with verse 31, this scene of the return of the "Son of man" who in verse 34, becomes a "king." (This signifies the setting up of a kingdom.) Here is what is interesting about His answer and at once telling. He has a king, (Himself) speaking to a future audience of Gentiles, and the "king" answers, **"To the extent that you did it unto one of the least of <u>these My</u> brethren."** Clearly indicates that <u>the brethren</u> He refers to are there present at His side! By saying, **"one of these"** without the writer naming names, it is also understood that either a gesture takes place or His listeners would know who "My brethren" were.

This prophecy is a reality which the Lord brings to pass in the spirit realm. This is a spiritually reality! Here in Matthew, the Lord is letting them know what would happen and wherever Matthew was read, everyone understood.

The narrative speaks of only four parties being present at this judgment,

1.) The Son of man (The king)
2.) The angels (Messengers)
3.) The Gentile sheep.
4.) The Gentile goats.

Who would you venture to guess might have been "His brethren? I have run upon many a believer who will reject correct Bible contextual reasoning when the answer challenges his or her beliefs. I'll be very frank with you; I have found that most Christians will side with their particular "sound doctrine" rather than the Bible. What they may see in the black and white Scripture will never have the validity upon their soul that their "beliefs" do! They will reason thusly, "I must not understand that correctly," or "It must be an error in the Bible 'because surely my denomination and/or the people who taught me cannot be wrong." However, the above is not such a "hard saying" therefore, most of you reading this would have no problem agreeing that the "angels" who "come with Jesus" have to be "His brethren." Furthermore, if the Gentiles who turned to Christ are the "sheep," than, the "angels/messengers" are entirely Hebrew believers who came to Christ. (These are the 144,000 – Revelation 7:4 and 14:1).

Now we must ask the question, When does the opportunity arise that those of the nations would "See" His brethren hungry, thirsty, a stranger, naked, sick or in prison?" Is this something future as some insist, or has there been a time when this possibly may have occurred in the past?

(Consider this)

Beginning around the year AD 44 with Acts chapter 13 onward the "brethren" of Jesus would began a mission westward sweeping across the Empire with the gospel in their hearts and on their lips. The Spirit commanded and they obeyed. Paul, Barnabus, Silas, Timothy, Apollo, Mark, Aquilla and Pricilla, and many, many others.

Saul/Paul

"I have been in labors, imprisonments, beaten, shipwrecked dangers, hardship, sleepless nights, hunger and thirst, cold and exposure." (2nd Corinthians 11:23-27)

The list of those who turned out to be "sheep" is long. They heard the message that the "brethren" of Jesus proclaimed and embraced it and the messenger. People like, Luke, Titus, Dionysius, Damaris, Phoebe, Epaenetus, and the list goes on in Romans chapter 16 and other places. They are referred to as "a great multitude" in Revelation 7:9. Many who do not want to accept the truth of Scripture have said, "Well yes, but it will be repeated, it is going to happen again." These, will acknowledge that some prophetic uttering has "seemed to be fulfilled" but must not have any meaning since Jesus has not returned in the flesh and the world has not physically ended. They, therefore, with no Bible backing go on to say that, <u>it is to be repeated in the future.</u> I have heard this preached for forty years.

For example, many erroneously view Daniel 11:31 as being fulfilled by a king named Epiphanes who forcefully intruded into the Holy of Holies in the second century BC when it is actually prophecy about AD 70. Therefore, when Jesus correctly quotes Daniel in Matthew 24:15, in reference to the Roman invasion of AD 70, the "futurist-prophecy-experts" claim Daniel 11:31 will be <u>fulfilled again.</u> Armed with this unbiblical mode of "second-fulfillments" whenever "prophecy-experts" have encountered prophecy which the Bible, other theologians, or history proves has been fulfilled in the past they glibly claim it has <u>a second</u> <u>fulfillment in the future.</u> By the way, there are three references to **"abomination of desolation"** in Daniel, (9:27, 11:31, and 12:11), all three refer to AD 70 and the Roman invasion and the destruction of the Temple. Further, it is to this time of AD 70 that the disciples all refer when they speak of the "end of the age!

<u>Verse 41- 43</u>

"Then He will say to those on His left, depart from me accursed ones, into the eternal fire which has been prepared for the devil and his angels. For I was hungry, and you gave me nothing to eat; I was thirsty, and you gave me nothing to drink; I was a stranger, and you did not invite me in; naked, and you did not clothe me; sick, and in prison, and you did not visit me."

The Jews who rejected Christ and His offer of eternal life through grace by faith in essence chose to be judged by the Law. Jesus had plainly warned the Jews in the light of day in Jerusalem.

"Do not think that I will accuse you before the Father; the one who accuses you is Moses, in whom you trust." (John 5:45)

When the "Great Tribulation" occurred in those seven terrible, years of devastation in Israel (AD 66 -73) God respected their wishes and judged them according to the Law. God had made the same offer to the "nations," that is, all the Gentiles, (non-Jews) across the Roman Empire, the civilized world of that time.

"For I am not ashamed of the gospel of Christ for it is the power of God for salvation to everyone who believes, to the Jew first and also to the Greek." (Romans 1:16)

Now, before Christ, allegorically at least, stood before all the Gentiles to whom the "offer of eternal life" had also been made. Many like Epaphroditus, and Clement, and women like Euodia and Syntyche "true comrades" and "fellow workers" with Paul, (Philippians 2:25 & 4:2-3) were among the "sheep," the "righteous." They were among those who responded affirmably to the gospel becoming part of many others had not responded to the gospel but instead had been among those who imprisoned, beat, and opposed the "brethren of Jesus." These unbelieving Gentiles like the Jews who rejected Christ had made their decision to be judged outside the blood of redemption, outside grace. They were "accursed" or "under curse" and unable to be received into (eternal) "life." "Eternal life" was imported onto human hearts not at AD 33 at Pentecost but AD 70-73 at the closing of the Old Covenant.

"Jesus said, Truly I say to you, there is no one who has left house or brothers or sisters, or mother or father or children or farms, for my sake and for the gospel's sake, but that he shall receive a hundred times as much now in the present age, houses and brothers and sisters and mothers and children and farms, along with persecutions, and in the age to come, eternal life." (Mark 10:29-30)

In Ephesians when the apostle Paul refers to the (age) "to come" (1:21), the Literal reads "impending," "To come" in Greek is Mello = "to be about to be or do." (Strong's' #3195). The disciples who wrote the New Testament were not in error concerning the "end of the age" (Read my book – "The Disciples and the Apocalypse.") The old age ended when the judgment by Law over Israel took place in the seven years of tribulation, AD 66-73.

Eternal Fire

Since this Matthew episode deals with the "end of the age," it should be without argument to say that "eternal fire" is a reference to the "lake of fire" from Revelation 19:20 & 20:15. How are we to take this description of the place of unbelievers? Should we accept the Catholic view from "Dante's Inferno," and one which Evangelicals mostly agree with? If damnation, hell and fire, were such a pertinent attendant of the gospel why are these elements not found in the writings of Paul? Paul writes of "wrath to come" but that refers to AD 66-73.

Judging

The "judging" which John has Jesus referring to in 5:22, 30 and 8:16 has to do with "separating" which is what the word "Judgment" means. It is the Greek word 'krisis' and that is precisely what Matthew 25 is all about.

Matthew 10:15, 12:36, 41 and 42.
Also 2 Peter 2:11 and Jude 9.

All refer to the judgment of Israel in AD 66-73. The parable of the "Ten Virgins," Matthew 25:1-13 is the judging or "dividing" of Israelites. The portion of Matthew 25 we are dealing with here is the "judging" or "dividing" of Gentiles. All this took place at the end of the "Great Tribulation" AD 66-73.

More On Eternal Fire

My guess is that the preaching of "hellfire" began much later when the gospel became corrupted by the priesthood of what came to be called the Catholic Church. I am not aware whether this can be proven one way or the other. However, the teaching of "eternal fire" is, scriptural; yet it needs to be understood spiritually because it is a spiritual act. One might have the inclination to think, "What is so difficult about understanding the phrase it seems to be cut and dried." However, if you will pardon the expression, this is precisely the human understanding "easy route" which has given Christianity a litany of unbiblical so-called "literal interpretations" which passes for "sound doctrine" among Evangelicalism.

The thinking of some is that if one does not interpret Scripture "literally" one is taking away from Scripture. People who insist on using a "literal" interpretation of prophecy throughout sincerely, if foolishly, believe they are protecting the integrity of the Book. In the meanwhile, their sincerity is doing serious damage to truth and to the practical life and mission of the Church.

While I do not mean to infer that one has to be highly educated to read the Bible I do mean one needs spiritual understanding. (Actually, much which passes for "education" has misled many). In the beginning of one of my high school years, we were taught a jingle in school which said, "Practice makes perfect." Weeks later, it was changed to, "Perfect practice makes perfect." Someone may say God made the Bible easy so the least layman can understand it. I believe this is true when it comes to salvation; however, beyond that the Lord would have us study and seek knowledge and revelation into the deeper things of God. There are segments of Scripture, especially prophecy, which, in the words of one of its writers, "are hard to be understood" (Second Peter 3:16). Furthermore, why would God place anointed ministries called "teachers" (Ephesians 4:11) if all one has to do is open the book and Walla! There it is!

I was born and raised in and around the cotton fields of South Texas to illiterate parents. My only credentials are that I am a called teacher of Scripture. Paul wrote, **"All are not teachers, are they?"** (1 Corinthians 12:29). Nonetheless, have you noticed that everyone is trying to be one? I am not an evangelist, apostle, or prophet, although I have been known to pastor a bit. What I know I know by revelation and what I've learned from other anointed teachers. Forty years of study are part of the equation however, I know one can study religiously and **"never come to the full knowledge of the truth"** (2 Timothy 3:7).

28

Without the Spirit's revelation all study does is increase head knowledge and "head knowledge puffs up," as Paul wrote. Now to get down to the business at hand. A look at two texts one in Hebrews and another in Isaiah are helpful in obtaining a biblical and spiritual perception of what the Bible means by "eternal fire."

"Our God is a consuming fire," (Hebrews 12:29).

"Who among us shall dwell with the <u>consuming fire</u>? Who among us shall dwell with <u>everlasting burning</u>? He who walks righteously, and speaks with sincerity." (Isaiah 33:14-15)

"Eternal fire" as we said above relates to the "lake of fire" of Revelation 19:20 and 20:15, which is called the "second death" in Revelation 20:14. Whether that "fire" consumes you or not, according to Isaiah, depends on your relationship with the Son of God. It seems the "righteous" will have no problem **"dwelling with consuming, everlasting fire."** Like firemen wearing Polyimide fiber type clothing and walking in the midst of flames. According to the commentaries, the word "consume," means "a total end," "dissolving," "cut off," and "melt." However, Revelation 20:10 says, the devil, the beast, and the false prophet thrown into the lake of fire will not have a "total end" but "will be tormented (there) day and night forever." All this seeming contradictory statements come about because of the human comprehension we have of Scripture. When we spiritually understand the lake of fire there are no contradictions.

Note that Revelation 20:6 reads,
"Blessed and holy is the one who has a part in the first resurrection; <u>over these the second death (lake of fire) has no power,</u> but they will be priests of God and of Christ and will reign with Him for a thousand years."

Two verses before we are introduced to two sets of individuals.

The first are:
"They set on thrones and judgment was given unto them. (Revelation 20:4a)

The second:
"I saw the souls of those who had been beheaded for the witness of Jesus." (Revelation 20:4b)

The first ones John sees sitting on the thrones and given judgment are physically alive since they are contrasted with the individuals mentioned immediately after who are referred to as "**souls who have been beheaded for the witness of Jesus.**" These ones sitting on thrones remind me very much of what the Lord told the apostles.

"Surely I say to you, in the regeneration when the Son of man shall sit in the throne of His glory, you also shall sit upon twelve thrones, judging the twelve tribes of Israel." (Matthew 19:28)

A key to comprehending the lake of fire is the fact that it is called the "second death" (Revelation 20:14). This is helpful because if we can know what the first death is than that will give us aid in possibly identifying the second. It has been taught that the "first death" is when the physical body dies. There is a popular saying among the Baptists for this teaching. "If you are born twice you will only die once and if you are only born once you will die twice." It is very catchy, however, I believe it misses the point altogether. As much as "literalists/Dispensationalists dislike the fact that some of us are "always trying to spiritualize the Scriptures" it is necessary to understand these "deaths" under a spiritual and biblical context.

The First Death

I believe all of us can agree that the "death" of the "lake of fire" is not physical but spiritual. Therefore, when the soul is cast into the "lake of fire" it would be the first time it is dying not the second. This is why I believe the "first death" occurs when the "First Adam" partook of the tree of the knowledge of good and evil. God told Adam that "on the day you eat thereof you shall surly die." Adam did and he did. Adam the soul man "died" on that very day as God had warned him; however, he died spiritually in soul not physically. That was the "first death" the "second death" in the lake of fire is likewise a spiritual/soul death! Therefore, it is to be understood in this context. The "first Adam," the soul-man "died" the first time in the garden. Those who refused to evolve into the "last Adam," the Spirit-man, but rather choose to remain in the image of the "first Adam" suffer a "second (soul) death."

The First Resurrection

Those of the "first resurrection" include two groups the "souls" indicated here in Revelation 20:4, who "come to life" or as the KJ has it, "live and reign." The second group are those who are physically alive and "set on thrones and judgment was given to them." The Lord spoke of the "souls" who were physically dead and were soon (Pentecost AD 33) to "live."

"Truly, truly, I say to you, an hour is coming and now is, when the dead shall hear the voice of the Son of God; and those who hear shall live." (John 5:25)
("Coming to life" or "live" should be understood as spiritual life and not as physical).

31

These "souls" are also referred to earlier in the Book of Revelation.

"When the lamb broke the fifth seal, I saw underneath the alter the souls of those who had been slain because of the word of God and because of their testimony. They cried out saying, how long, Lord, will you refrain from judging and avenging our blood on those who dwell on the earth. <u>There was given to each of them a white robe;</u> and they were told to rest a little while longer, until their fellow servants and their brethren who were to be killed even as they had been, should be completed also." (Revelation 6:9-11)

These "souls" were "given life," (white robes) at the start of regeneration on the day of Pentecost AD 33. The second group in the "first resurrection" included the twelve who were "given thrones and they set on them" along with the one hundred and twenty and subsequently all of those who came to Christ up until AD 73. This is indicated in a conversation the Lord had with those who followed him shortly before His betrayal and arrest.

"After a little while the world will behold me no more; but you will behold me; because I live, you shall live also." (John 14:19)

The way I understand this is all who died in faith (In Abraham) prior to the cross, and all who believed in Christ between AD 33 and AD 73, including Gentiles belong to the "first resurrection." At the **"great white throne judgment"** in AD 73 all of the rest the living and the dead, **"were judged according to their deeds."**

These had not come to know Christ as Savior some had even died before Christ, yet according to Scripture, some of them were nonetheless **"written in the book of life"** (Revelation 20:11-15). The "Lake of fire" had power, (jurisdiction) over this second group in that their spiritual "destination" was still, up in the air, much as a court of law has power (jurisdiction) over a defendant on trial. These of the second group were not being presumed guilty but were being investigated through the "books" where some of them were indeed found "guilty."

"If anyone's name was not found written in the book of life, he was thrown into the lake of fire" (Revelation 20:15).

Verse 41b

Devil and his Angels

What some people have concluded from the phrase **"which has been prepared for the devil and his messengers"** is to think that this "eternal fire" was not meant for humanity. The thinking here seems to be that God was not prepared for gospel rejecters. Moreover, since He was not prepared for unbelieving humans that is where He had to cast them. This thinking also desires to give the impression that God is so loving that He never intended to punish humans in the first place, thus, the lack of a place to do it in, and the necessity of having to use a place designed for the devil, i.e., "fallen angels." I believe God is always prepared, He knows the beginning from the end in all matters and in every situation. He is not like the U.S. Marines He never has to improvise.

Therefore, before we sell out entirely to the idea that this "fire" was for "fallen angels" we should consider for a moment the possibility that the "devil" may not even be a "fallen angel." The word "devil" which means "accuser" is the correct term here. This term is only found in the New Testament by the way. The term Satan which means "Adversary" is found in the Old and the New Testament and while both terms may refer to the same entity, they indicate different aspects of that entity.

"The great dragon was thrown down, the serpent of old who is called the devil and Satan" (Revelation 12:9a)

I quote the above text so you will have at your mental disposal all the titles of this character. In the Old Testament book of Numbers, it is recorded.

"The people spoke against God and Moses, and the Lord sent fiery serpents among the people and they bit the people and they died. Moses interceded for the people and the Lord told Moses to make a bronze serpent and to set it on a standard that when anyone is bitten when he looks at it, he shall live." (Numbers 21:5-9)

Jesus likened this "serpent on the standard" to Himself being lifted up on the cross.

"As Moses lifted up the serpent in the wilderness, even so must the Son of man be lifted up that whosoever believes in Him may have eternal life." (John 3:14, 15)

Now add this text to the equation.
"Our old man (life) was crucified with Christ" (Romans 6:6a).

The cross was crowded on that eventful Friday.
Serpent = Jesus on Cross = Old man.

Now consider the following three statements which will offer more light to what we discussed in verse 32.
 1. **"That our <u>body of sin</u> might be done away with (**made powerless**)."** (Romans 6:6b)

2. **"Who will set me free from the <u>body of death?"</u>** (Romans 7:24)

3. **"Jesus partook of the same <u>flesh and blood</u> as us that through death He might render powerless <u>him who had the power of death</u>, that is, the devil."** (Hebrews 2:14

   What is the "body of sin?" What does Paul mean by the "body of death?" These refer to "flesh and blood" which in turn refers to man in his "soulish nature" composed of soul aided by the physical body. Paul refers to this man when he writes to the Corinthians.

"But the <u>natural man</u> (soulish man) does not receive the things of the Spirit (1 Corinthians 2:14).

   "Natural" is the Greek word 'psuchikos,' which in English is "soulish" [Strong's #5591], its root is the Greek word 'psuche' which is "soul" [Strong's 5590]. Therefore, the term "natural man" is correctly interpreted "soulish man" in the Concordant Literal New Testament. This "soulish man" is "flesh and blood," "body of sin," and "body of death." This is the "old man" Christ wore or took with Him on the cross. The "soul man" or "old man" is composed of body and soul.

"The Lord God formed man of <u>dust</u> from the ground, and <u>breathed</u> into his nostrils the breath of life; and man became a living soul" (Genesis 2:7).

The Lord took both of these entities up on the cross to crucify them. Our "soul" [self-will, carnal emotions, and feelings] was "put to death" with the intent that **"we too** (the soul man) **might walk in newness of life"** (Romans 6:4c).

It is of the utmost importance that we understand that the spiritual is what the reality is.

"He who raised Christ Jesus from the dead will also <u>give life to your</u> <u>mortal bodies</u>" (Romans 8:11).

If we were to give the above a so called "literal' interpretation and say that Paul is speaking of the physical body we would be interpreting out of context. Why? Because in the preceding verse, number ten, Paul has just said that, the "body" of physically alive believers were "dead" Therefore, we know he is not writing of physical death why than would we think that "giving (them) life" in the next verse, means physical life? After all, the bodies of the believers he was writing to were already physically alive! Furthermore, in that verse ten Paul states, **"The body is dead because of sin."** What sin? Were they not washed away by the blood of the lamb? The way Futurists/Dispensationalists have ran rough- shod through that question is to teach that the physical body still sins therefore, it will not receive immortality until the day of resurrection. However, the context as we have shown is not speaking of the physical body!

36

The word "mortal" is an adjective describing the believers' condition as to their life in Adam, i.e., the first creation. That old man was "dead" in Christ but would receive "life" and enter into immortality (newness of life) with the "life-giving Spirit" to "bear the image of the heavenly" (1 Corinthians 15:45 & 49).

Back to the Devil.

When Jesus hung on the cross and all our sins were placed on Him – **"He (God) made Him (Jesus) who knew no sin <u>to</u> <u>be sin</u> for us"** (2 Corinthians 5:21a). When Jesus hung on the cross, He became that serpent. Now everyone who "looks up at Him" lives, forevermore. I will put it to you tenderly, when Jesus was on the cross, He became "devilish man" **"to loose us from the <u>works</u> (acts) of that devil (ish man)"** (1 John 3:8c). **"In Him we were also circumcised with a circumcision made without hands, in the removal of the body of the flesh by the circumcision (death) of Christ."** (Colossians 2:11). Jesus is no longer on the cross but His substituent act on humanity's behalf is eternal.

Religion teaches us that upon Adam's initial encounter with the serpent, (Genesis 3) man relinquished his authority and came under the dominion of Satan. We are told that from that point on man begin to do evil because he is under that dominion. This reminds me of a popular TV comedian named Flip Wilson who used to crack the entire nation up by admitting to some wrong doing during his monologue and than saying, "The devil made me do it." What we all thought hilarious was his blaming another entity for what was obviously something he himself was guilty of. I believe what the Scriptures are actually relating to us concerning this matter is that man through his self-will gave birth to the devil.

37

Moreover, I propose to you that man did not relinquish his God-given authority but was tempted by evil (evil coming out of the thoughts and intents of the heart) once he walked into the arena of self-driven purposes. Evil is born out of man's heart and is manifested by wars, murders, betrayals, perversions, and greed.

(First – Evil comes out of the heart of man)
"Out of the heart (of man) come malicious reasoning, rationalizations, murders, adulteries, sexual immorality, thefts, false witness, and slanders" (Matthew 15:19).

(Paul writes)
"I find then the principle (law) that <u>evil is present in me, the one who wishes to do good.</u>" (Romans 7:21).

The Lord is giving us the source of evil and activity. He says it is the heart of man. If the first Adam merely had a "fall," why was a second Adam necessary, why not just "straighten up" the first one? Paul informs us by revelation that the first Adam was only a "type of Him who was to come." (Romans 5:14) The word "type" is the Greek word 'tupos;' "element of a parable or model of some reality which was yet to appear." (Strong's Lexical Aids # 5179). The reality "which was yet to appear" was Jesus. In the perfect plan of the Creator the "model" was made with free or self-will which he took full use of in following Eve into becoming "wise;" "intelligent knowledge of the reason." (Strong's # 7919). I do not know what else the devil may be in biblical context but a "fallen angel" he never was.

Old Man = First Adam

Reason has its uses as well as its abuses. Reason as desirable as it may be has its limits faith does not. Reason can not only lead us into fleshly sin but even into denying a Creator. Reason can not cause you (a soul man) to be "conformed, assimilated, or fashioned like unto Jesus" (Romans 8:29). Once an individual (soul man) comes to faith in Christ, he becomes a "new man" (2 Corinthians 5:17). He (soul man) should now "walk in newness of life" (Romans 6:4). The life we lived in the "soul man" (first Adam) is now called the "old man" or "old self" and was "crucified with Christ" (Romans 6:6). As we may have noted before, that "soul-man" we are in the first Adam is "quickened" or in modern English "given life" at the end of the judgment of Israel. The judgment lasted seven years from AD 66 until AD 73. This is what Paul is explaining to the Roman believers when he writes. "We wait eagerly for the redemption of our body" (Romans 8:23b).

As I said earlier, Futurists/Dispensationalists would take Paul to be saying the physical bodies of believers will be resurrected in the future. However, if we look at how Paul is using the words "body" "died" and "flesh" within the context of Romans chapters six through eight we will readily be able to tell this is not so.

"Our old man (soul man) was crucified with Him, that our <u>body</u> (of sin) might be done away with" (Romans 6:6). (Body = Old Man, not physical body).

"For while we <u>were in the flesh</u>" (Romans 7:5).

Paul is saying believers "were" in the flesh." "Were" is past tense, therefore, by "flesh" Paul was not referring to their physical bodies because the believers he is writing to are presently in their physical bodies as Paul writes!

(Flesh = the sinful condition of the soul man, body and soul, in his rebellion against God.) The life we lived in Adam, the soul man, was a "fleshly" life (no spiritual power) it was weak and therefore, unable to either obey God or resist sin, it was devilish. (Romans 8:2).

"But now we have been released from the Law, <u>having died</u> to that by which we were bound" (Romans 7:6).

"Died" as you can tell does not refer to literal physical death but to who we were in our old man who died on the cross with Christ.

"But I am of flesh, sold into bondage to sin" (Romans 7:14).

Here Paul begins to explain how an Israelite (note 7:1) who did not know Christ lived on the inside. The Israelite knew the Law and in his mind, (thinking) he apprehended its goodness, its truth; however, he was only a soul man, (no spiritual power) to overcome the impulses of the weakness and attraction to evil. Paul was not speaking of his present condition at the time, he was not saying that he, "was doing the very thing he hated" (Romans 7:15). That would have been preposterous. Paul was a man led of the Spirit who lived his Christian life in obedience to the Lord. This is not two natures in conflict.

"If Christ is in you though the <u>body is dead</u>" (Romans 8:10).

We can readily tell that Paul does not mean that the physical bodies of those in Christ were physically or literally dead. The "body" refers to the soul man (old man) who was crucified with Christ. Therefore, when Paul writes in 8:23 that, **"we are waiting eagerly for the redemption of our body"** we know by the context that he is not referring to his physical body. The soul man, "first Adam" was to be "given life" (Romans 8:11) to be united with the "Last Adam, the life-giving Spirit" and enter into new and Spiritual life! Someone may ask, whether Paul and all believers didn't already have spiritual life since Paul tells the Corinthians,

"If any man be in Christ, he is a new creation" (2 Corinthians 5:17a).

Here I will again let Paul explain.

"The <u>spirit is alive,</u> but <u>the body,</u> (old man, who we were in Adam) is dead. But God will give life to our <u>mortal bodies,</u> (the soul man who was subject to dying) through His Spirit" (Romans 8:10 &11).

The source of evil and sin is the lust in the heart of man. **"Each man is tempted when he is carried away and enticed <u>by his own lust.</u> Then when lust has conceived, it gives birth to sin; and when sin is accomplished, it brings forth death"** (James 1:14-15).

"But now you also, put them all aside; anger, wrath, malice, slander, and abusive speech from your mouth. Do not lie to one another, since you laid aside the old self (man) with its <u>evil works</u>" (Colossians 3:8, 9).

41

Verses 44-45

"Lord when did we see you hungry, or thirsty, or a stranger, or naked, or sick, or in prison, and did not take care of you? Then He will answer them, saying, to the extent that you did not do it to one of the least of these, (Jewish Christian Evangelists, AD 33-73) you did not do it to me."

By this question, we can see that those who rejected the "brethren" of the Lord will "recognize" the Lord of Lords. Neither "sheep" nor "goats" were aware that God expects mankind to "hear" by their heart and not their brain. The heart has spiritual "ears" and "eyes" and therefore, can "hear," "perceive," and "know" in a spiritual level. All of us should be keenly aware of this in our daily living, lest we also continually miss God. God even expected spiritually dead citizens of the Roman Empire to "hear" the gospel.

"So faith from hearing, and hearing by the word of Christ" (Romans 10:17).

Notice, the text has two parts. The Spirit of the spoken Word (Rhema) has power to create faith or persuasion into accepting God's word as true. Secondarily, which comes first, our heart is able to "spiritually hear" because of the intrinsic power of the Word. Whether one accepts or rejects God's invitation into salvation is the decision of the soul. Nevertheless, we can "hear" and we can believe. Therefore, we are without excuse.

Verse 46

Eternal Punishment

"These will go away into <u>eternal punishment,</u> but the righteous into <u>eternal life.</u>"

"Eternal punishment," one would assume takes place in the "eternal fire" which was discussed in verses 41-43. Here we are told what the "fire" entails. The Greek word for "punishment" is 'kolasis,' Strong's (2851). Here is what the Strong's commentary has to say.

(Strong's commentary)
"Distinguished from 'timoria (5098), the vindictive character of the punishment as the predominant thought which satisfies the inflictor's sense of outraged justice as defending his own honor or that of the violated law. 'Kolasis,' on the other hand, <u>conveys the notion of punishment for the correction and bettering of the offender.</u>"

To be fair to you the reader I will now relate the rest of Strong's commentary on this word. However, I will do so with this prologue. Dr. Strong gives no textual, biblical, proof or reason for this added commentary. This leads one, of a suspicious mind like me, to believe he is only doing so to "push" his particular leanings or understanding of the word. I am not accusing Dr. Strong of being dishonest but perhaps he may be, as it seems, unbiblical. With that said, here is the rest of what his commentary says.

(Further Strong commentary)
"It does not always, however, have the same meaning in the N. T. for example in Matthew 25:46 'kolasis- aionios' does not refer to temporary corrective punishment and discipline, but has more the meaning of 'timoria' punishment."

Here is my problem. Dr. Strong first gives us the meaning of the Greek word 'kolasis.' Than he follows that by saying, that in Matthew 25:46 the word does not mean what he just said it means. Notice the good Dr. adds "temporary" to his last part of the commentary saying, "kolasis does not refer to temporary corrective punishment and discipline in Matthew 25:46." However, in the first part when he gives us the meaning sans any personal thoughts the word "temporary" is nowhere to be found. What this leads me to believe is that the word "eternal" (aionios) in Matthew is throwing him off kilter. Dr. Strong seems to be reasoning thusly, any "punishment (which would be) for the correction and betterment of the offender" is not eternal but ends when the offender is "corrected," therefore, since Jesus is saying that this punishment is "eternal" it cannot be 'kolasis' even if it says 'kolasis."

To begin with there are only two places where the word 'kolasis' is used which leaves a very small margin for error in its usage. Secondly, why would Matthew use 'kolasis' when he meant 'timoria?' It seems to me that the biblical way to go at this is not to twist the meaning of a word supposing it means other that what it does but rather to challenge our understanding of the text. For instance, instead of trying to change the word, change your perspective of how you view "eternal." Some may think, "eternal is eternal you cannot change it!" However, I am not suggesting that we change it but rather how we view its usage.

What I mean is the "fire" and its "punishing" effect may be "eternal," it will always exist but does it necessarily follow that those being "punished" will be there eternally? I believe to let 'kolasis' say what it means and mean what it says is the biblical way. I mentioned above that the word 'kolasis' is found in only two places in the N. T. One you already know which is here in Matthew 25:46, the other is in the first epistle of John.

"There is no fear in love; but perfect love casts out fear, because <u>fear involves punishment</u>" (1 John 4:18).

Understanding that this "punishment" in John and the one in Matthew are the same word 'kolasis,' helps us to perceive that the "punishment" that "fear" has is the same "punishment" that the "lake of fire" has. Therefore, if we determine what kind of "punishment" "fear" has we can know what the "punishment" of "eternal fire" is. We know this much, fear in a heart can and usually conceives, in one degree or another, anxiety, phobias, nervousness, depression, inferiority complexes that lead to loneliness, hate toward peers, murder, physical ailments and death. What I am saying is the "Punishment" of "fear" is the absence of peace, love, joy, happiness, and comfort; it is the unsoundness of soul and body. The result is that the connection of "fear" and the "lake of fire" can be clearly seen here.

"I heard the sound of thee in the garden and I <u>feared.</u>" (Genesis 3:10)

The result of the "First Death" in the Garden was "fear" which has or <u>is "punishment"</u>
The result of the "Second Death" has or <u>is "punishment."</u>

45

First death = kolasis.
Second death = kolasis

There is another illustration of this word 'Kolasis' from "Young's Analytical Concordance to the Bible." Dr. Young says the word means "restraint," I am very much in agreement with this. The "devil," the "beast," and the "false prophet," are entities who will never exit the "punishment" of the lake of fire. They will never breathe free air nor see the light of day ever again and here is why.

"The devil was thrown into the lake of fire and brimstone, where the beast and the false prophet are also; and they will be tormented <u>day and night forever and ever"</u> (Revelation 20:10).

The beast and the false prophet are the political dynasty founded under the authority of the "First Adam." The "beast" is not a future antichrist. The "beast" was the four world empires of the "age of the first Adam." They arose onto the world stage under the mandate given to Adam, (Genesis 1:28).

Babylon
Mede-Persia
Greece
Rome

They are history and will forever remain so. The "age of the soul-man Adam" is ended. We are citizens of the "age of the Spirit-man/Last Adam," Jesus Christ. This is why every would-be world conqueror since the end of Rome has met with dismal failure. There will never be another world empire unless it rules under the flag of Jesus Christ.

I believe it is the intent of the Almighty that benign civil governments rule the world under the influence of Christian values, morals, and compassion. There have been notable failures among us of those who would rule the world with a sword or gun. These types of world empires ruled by brutal force are under eternal "restraint" never to be seen again. This is why the Soviet Union expired with a whimper with no shots being fired. Below is a list of some more.

1. Beginning immediately after the collapse of the last "First Adam" Empire (Roman) and for centuries thereafter not all the kings of the so-called "Holy Roman Empire" along with the best efforts of the "Mother Church" could cobble together an empire. This is what prompted the composition of that well known ditty.

"Humpty-Dumpty set on a wall,
Humpty-Dumpty had a great fall,
All the king's horses and all the king's men
Could not put Humpty-Dumpty together again."

2. Napoleon Bonaparte

"Napoleon bit off more then he could chew,
Then at once, before he knew,
England said, how do you do,
Let's meet us two at Waterloo."

3. Hitler-Mussolini- Hirohito

"The unholy trinity of greed,
Who with bluster, gun, and speed.
Rushed to make the world bleed,
Met with Ike and Nimitz's fleet."

4. Marx-Lenin-Stalin

"They had the perfect plan,
Kill everyone you can,
Build your castles on the sand,
And put your trust in man."

Devil - Restraint

The entity known as the "devil" will also remain under eternal "restraint." The "being bound" and being "thrown into the abyss" or as the King James has it "bottomless pit" for a "thousand years" is also a "restraint," albeit a temporary one (Revelation 20:1-3). This "temporary restraint" "so that he could not deceive the nations" for that period, has been called the "Pax Romana" by secular historians. It means the "Roman Peace" noted for the harmony and scarcity of war during those years. Of course the historians do not attribute the "peace" to the restraint of the devil they simply note it. There are two aspects to the "restraint" in the Lake of fire.

"The one who practices sin (sins habitually) is of the devil; for the devil sins from the beginning" (1 John 3:8).

The linage of the "First Adam" is in mind here. All humanity was "of the devil." That "serpent/Old (Adam) Man "was crucified with Christ" (Romans 6:6), But that "natural," soul-man is brought back from that "death" (spiritual) by resurrection to "be united" with the "life–giving Spirit-man."

"For if we have been united with Him (Jesus) in the likeness of His death, we shall also be united in the likeness of His resurrection" (Romans 6:5).

The "old-man, natural, <u>devilish life</u> is "cast into the lake of fire" to remain under "restraint" forever more. This is the first aspect of this "restraint. The second follows from this first one it being that the "devil" is now "judged" and "cast out" of authority no longer to "rule" or build empires.

"Now judgment is upon this world; now the ruler of this world shall be cast out" (John 12:31).

"When he (Holy Spirit) comes He will convict the world concerning judgment, because the ruler of this world has been judged" (John 16:8 &11).

Verse 46a

Eternal Life

The "righteous enter eternal life."

The king is here dispensing "life eternal" to the "sheep." This is to be differentiated from "being given white robes" (Revelation 6:11) and "they came to life" (Revelation 20:4). The "white robes and the "life" given in these two instances refer to the "spirits of (Hebrew) just men made perfect." (Hebrews 12:23). They along with physically alive (also Hebrew) believers who "set on thrones" are the "first resurrection." However, neither yet had received "eternal life."

Eternal life is given when the age of the "soul-man" ends and the age of the Life-giving "Spirit-man" (Jesus) commences in AD 73. The "age of the soul-man" begins with the creation of the "First Adam" in Genesis and ends in the "fullness of times" in AD 73.

The "age of the Spirit-man" (Last Adam) begins in AD 73 with the judgment of Israel and the Roman Empire. At that time, sin was judged and "death" ended initiating "eternal life," when law ends so does (Soul) "death." (The "death" that Adam died upon disobedience in the garden.)

"The sting of death is (was) sin, and the power of sin is (was) the law." (1 Corinthians 15:56)

"Christ is the end of the law for righteousness." (Romans 10:4)

Grace and law ran concurrently from AD 33 until AD 73. The Lord gave forty years for the "gospel to be preached in all the "inhabited earth" (Roman Empire) and then the end came" (Matthew 24:14). The law was satisfied when Jesus hung on the cross and every soul who accepted the sacrifice of the Son God through the preaching of the disciples was spared judgment. Between AD 66 and AD 73, the judgment of the Law was unleashed in "fiery judgment." In Israel, it was the invasion of the Roman Legions, whose fury against the Jewish rebellion (apostasy) (2 Thessalonians 2:3) devastated the entire country, burning Jerusalem and destroying the Temple. Across the Empire, it was civil war between June 68 and July 69 as mighty heads rolled including those of four successive Emperors.

Nero = Committed suicide as Roman rebels gave chase.
Galba = Lynched in the Forum in Rome.
Otho = Committed suicide upon being defeated in battle.
Vitellius = Killed during battle in Rome.

The Age To Come

"Jesus said to them, Truly I say to you, there is no one who has left house or wife or brothers or parents or children, for the sake of the kingdom of God. Who will not receive many times as much at this time <u>and in the age to come,</u> eternal life." (Luke 18:29-30)

When the Lord spoke this promise to the disciples the "age too come" was still forty years in the future. He used the Greek word 'erchomai' Strong's (2064) which is the regular word one would use for something not immediate.

The apostle Paul writing to the Ephesians possible as late as AD 64, two years before the "Great Tribulation" was to begin mentions **"the age to come"** also. However, Paul uses a different Greek word for **"come"** because the "new age" was upon them.

"God has raised Christ far above all rule and authority and power and dominion and every name that is named, not only in this age but also in <u>the one to come."</u> (Ephesians 1:20-21)

Paul used the Greek word 'mello' Strong's ((3195) meaning, "about to do something, about to be" An English word for this phrase today is the word **"impending"** and this is precisely the word that the "Concordant Literal New Testament" uses.

"Not only in this age but also in that which is impending."

Paul is referring to this "new age" when he writes to the Roman Church.

"This, also do, being aware of the era, that it is already the hour for us to be roused out of sleep, for now is our salvation nearer than when we believe(ed). (Romans 13:11) Concordant Literal New Testament).

"Eternal life" has not a thing to do with the physical body. The word "life" is the Greek word 'Zoë "referring to the principle of life in the spirit and soul" Strong's (2222). The Greek word for life of the physical body is 'bios,' Strong's (979). The word "eternal" is the Greek word 'Aionios,' Strong's (166). This same word is used by Paul when speaking of God.

"According to the commandment of the <u>eternal God</u>" (Romans 16:26).

This "eternal life" could not be given to believers until Christ "married the Church" (Revelation 19:7-9). Upon His death and resurrection, AD 33, Christ (God) was loosed from His marriage to Israel but Christ would not marry the Church until all of the inhabited earth (The Roman Empire) was given opportunity through the gospel to become part of His bride. The invitations were sent out for forty years and while this was transpiring, His first wife Israel now a widow kept insisting she was the chosen.

"How much she has glorified herself, and lived luxuriously, so much torment and sorrow give her; for she says in her heart, I sit a queen <u>and am no widow</u>, and shall see no sorrow" (Revelation 18:7).

She had been rejected and was not aware, the times they were a-changing. Sorrow and torment came upon her through the "Great Tribulation" AD 66 through AD 73. The Church is now in the Spirit-man-age, which is eternal (Ephesians 3:21), and there is no turning back the clock towards unbelieving Israel. Any individual whether Jew or Gentile can come to Christ today and become part of the Church of God. However, as to those Christians today who favor Israel believing Scripture promises a future especially for Jews I have only one thing to say, you are greatly mistaken!

"Eternal life" came to the Church through the "Parousia" (presence) of the Lord among His people. It is a spiritual presence, since the Lord is a Spirit. I heard a preacher on the radio once who said that the Lord is in heaven with a "glorified" physical body and still bearing the wounds from the nails and spear. I pray at least some of you view that statement as insidiously blasphemous. I think that Bible knowledge like this radio preacher's is as splendid an example of biblical ignorance as can be found. Because **"The Word was made flesh"** (soul and body) **and dwelt among us"** (John 1:14), and that Word (soul/body) arose from death and returned to its eternal glory.

"Now O Father, glorify thou me with thin own self with the glory which I had with you before the world was." (John 17:5).

Most Christians have forgotten that our physical bodies unlike the Lord's are "dust of the ground" (Genesis 2:7) not destined for life everlasting.

"Then shall the dust return to the earth as it was: and the spirit shall return unto God who gave it." (Ecclesiastes 12:7).

Most, and sad to say, guided by seminary instructed commentators, fail to examine Scripture thoroughly such as the one in Daniel.

"Many of those who sleep in the <u>dust of the ground</u> will awake some to everlasting life and some to everlasting shame" (Daniel 12:2).

First, we should determine what "asleep" is.

<u>Is it the spirit?</u>
It could not be the spirit because our spirit returns to God upon physical death.

<u>Is it the soul?</u>
No, you say because it says "dust" and "ground."
<u>Is it the physical body?</u>
Yes, you say, it has to be speaking of our physical bodies.

The messenger is speaking to Daniel of centuries of the deceased and it would be seven hundred more years before the resurrection was to occur, some say it has still not occurred. So why would the messenger say they were asleep? If these are physical bodies, they are past sleeping already dust, nothing!

Note also that these **"sleep in the dust of the ground"** includes saints. Nonetheless, Jesus when confronted by the Sadducees concerning the resurrection quotes God speaking to Moses concerning the patriarchs who had been dead for 350 years.

"God spoke unto Moses saying, I am the God of Abraham, Isaac, and Jacob. He is not the God of the dead, but the <u>God of the living;</u> you therefore do greatly err" (Mark 12:26-27).

Among these in the "dust of the ground" are the Patriarchs, David, Moses, and the prophets. Since many of you are still anticipating a physical resurrection we would have to include the twelve apostles, Paul, Stephen, Luke, Mark, Mary Magdalene, who have been dead for two thousand years. Here is my point, if all of these are "dust in the ground" and who by now have become nothing how is God then the "God of the living and not the dead? Some might say it is only their physical bodies which are "dust of the ground" their spirits are alive and therefore, God is "God of the living." My answer to them would be, one moment please; you can't have your cake and eat it too. The Scripture plainly reads,

"Many of <u>them that sleep</u> in the dust of the ground shall awake.

It does not say, "<u>Their bodies</u> are asleep in the dust of the ground." It is "them" who sleep! Furthermore, what do physical bodies have to do with "everlasting shame" only a soul can experience shame. Our body could be in Timbuktu and our soul in Jupiter and feel ashamed. Alternatively, our physical body could be where the soul is and still feel no shame. I propose to you that what are "asleep in the dust of the ground" are souls. A look at the Hebrew words and their usage may alleviate some doubt and pain.

According to "Cruden's Complete Concordance" "Dust denotes likewise the grave and death."

"Then the Lord God said to the serpent, and dust shall you eat all the days of your life." (Genesis 3:14)

Do you think that serpents eat dust? The picture that comes to mind is that a snake slinks across the ground and if the ground is dusty, some is bound to get in its mouth. David uses the word in the Psalms.

"Thou does lay me in the <u>dust of death</u>" (Psalm 22:15).

Is it possible that "dust" could be symbolic of spiritual or soul death? I think so, especially when we look at the word "ground."

"Ground"

The Hebrew word for "ground" or "earth" in Daniel 12:2, is 'Adamah' = "earth, ground, land." "<u>It is clearly derived from the root Adam,</u>" Strong's (127). The Lexicon goes on to say, "The body of the first man Adam was formed from 'adamah."

Therefore, as far as my understanding of the New Testament concerning the teaching of physical resurrection goes what the heavenly messenger is telling Daniel is this.

"Many of them that sleep in the <u>death</u> (dust) <u>of Adam</u> (ground) shall awake."

The "first Adam" was a soul-man. He "died" in the day that he ate thereof." The "many who are sleep in the dust of the ground" are Hebrews, the people of Israel. Some died faithful some died faithless. When God was to "gather His people in Christ," including Gentiles, (Ephesians 1:10) the faithless would rise to shame and the faithful to life-everlasting. All of these Hebrews to whom the divine messenger refers "asleep in the dust of the ground" had "died the death of Adam." This is to say, they died as all men, and they went "the way of all flesh" the faithful to the **"bosom of Abraham"** the faithless across the great divide in Hades, (Luke 16:19-23). Therefore, they were all "asleep in the death of Adam."

56

In the resurrection all the faithful soul-men "**dead in Christ shall rise first**" (as "spiritual-men," (1 Thessalonians 4:16). The faithless soul-men were not destined to graduate into "eternal (spiritual) life," at least not before a detour through the "lake of fire" (Revelation 20:15). We, (believers) "**shall all be changed**" (souls' condition), (1 Corinthians 15:51 &52). Eternal Life was given to believing souls at the commencement of the "Spirit-man age," AD 73. At that time all soul-men physically alive or dead who had come to Christ or died in faith were "raised from the dead" (from the death of the cross) (AD 73) and were "united" with the "Spirit-Man" (Christ Jesus). It is the natural, soul-man man which was "mortal," that is, was subject to spiritual death, now coming into "deathlessness," which is to say, no longer subject to "death." Paul phrases it this way, "**when this mortal puts on immortality,**" (1 Corinthians 15:54). This is "eternal life!"

"**Therefore, my brethren, be steadfast, immovable, always abounding in the work of the Lord, knowing that your toil is not in vain in the Lord.**" (1 Corinthians 15:58).

Considering that I take the "judgment of the nations" as fulfilled prophecy some may ask "what about judgment today or in the future?" The answer is this: The "great white throne judgment" of AD 73 was an "all at once" judgment to close out the books on the old creation of the soul-man. The world was still under the "law of sin and death" (except for the saved) (Romans 8:2). Grace and Law ran concurrently from AD 33 until AD 73 and all who entered the "ark," that is Christ, during that period were "saved from the wrath to come" (Matthew 3:7). In AD 66 the "wrath" was released (Revelation 9:14), the "four angels" mentioned there refer to the four "messengers" which are Exodus, Leviticus, Numbers, and Deuteronomy.

The Law, when not fulfilled by an individual to the letter (and no one but Christ ever did), promised death. The only thing which held the "wrath" at bay was the "daily sacrifice" in the Temple which "covered," but did not eliminate the sins of Israel! In August of AD, 70 as the Temple set surrounded by Roman Legions the "daily sacrifice" ended for lack of priests [or lambs], (Josephus, "The Essential Works" Pg. 364, by Paul L. Maier. After AD 73, what has ended is the "wrath of the Law" and God's anger concerning sin. The world after AD 73 is under the auspices of grace altogether! God's anger was spent on Christ on the cross. So what about judgment today? Judgment, for loss or reward is an ongoing process for believers by "sowing and reaping" (Galatians 6:7), and the "punishment of fear" (Lake of fire) for the Christ rejecters.

To be continued.

Material available from the Author

Other Books (English)

"Israel-No Longer Chosen" $11.99

"Regeneration and New Creation" $7.95

"Disciples and the Apocalypse" $7.95

Books (Spanish)

¿"Vendrá Un Líder Mundial Llamado Anticristo?" $9.95

"Ya fuimos Sanados" $2.95

Full catalog available

Write - cityofglorymc@aol.com

Visit – www.cogmc.net

Address
P.O. Box 240608
San Antonio, Tx. 78224

City of Glory Miracle Center - where I pastor is located at 19540 S. US Hwy. 281 San Antonio, Texas.

Services

Sunday - 10:30 am

Monday - Bible Study 7 pm

Notes

Notes

Notes

Notes

www.ingramcontent.com/pod-product-compliance
Lightning Source LLC
Chambersburg PA
CBHW071024040426
42443CB00007B/919